The Diary of an Everyday Christian

by

Ann Lovett Baird

The Diary of an Everyday Christian
Copyright 2010
by
Ann Lovett Baird
Cover design by Matthew Wells

ISBN (13-digit) 978-1-934335-27-7
ISBN (10-digit) 1-934335-27-4

Special Delivery Books
46561 State Highway 118
Alpine, TX 79830

Printed in the United States of America
All rights reserved. No part of this book may be reproduced or transmitted in any form by any means, electrical or mechanical, including photography, recording, or by any information or retrieval system without written permission of the author, except for the inclusion of brief quotations in reviews.

Dedication

I dedicate this book to my sister, Jane, who prayed the first prayer with me—the prayer that forever changed my relationship with God. For in that prayer, she introduced me to Jesus Christ as my personal savior, and I started a daily journey with Him. Without God's strength, I could not have survived some of the events that have happened in my life.

I also wish to dedicate this book to my friend, Denalyn, whose kindness, acceptance and preciousness have helped me through some of the most challenging times in my life. She is always a spark of hope and inspiration for my walk in faith. As I watch her sing in church, I see her totally immersed in praise and adoration for our Lord. The Lord's love shines through her sense of humor, spiritual strength and kindness.

Introduction

A friend of mine once described me as imperfectly perfect. Indeed, God uses my imperfection most. In this diary I don't intend to tell other Christians how to live. Only God can guide each Christian in a daily walk and relationship with Him. Instead, I view this diary as a collection of reflections of a very humble Christian walking with the Lord one day at a time. I have often stumbled, bruised my knee, and cried to Him because I needed someone to help me up.

I pray that *The Diary of an Everyday Christian* will inspire other Christians in their journey with Christ each day, and that God will give readers a message through these pages, whether a small encouragement or a new insight. God always makes Himself available to us when we're ready to notice Him. In this book, the passages in italics are prayers and conversations offered to the Lord. I hope they will help you on your journey with Him.

Ann Lovett Baird

The First Prayer

The life of the Christian begins with the first prayer to God in the person of Jesus Christ who gives His grace and gift of eternal life. The prayer goes something like this: "I am human, Lord, and I have sinned against You. You have graciously sent Your son, Jesus, to die for my sins so that I might have eternal life. I ask for forgiveness for my sins and invite You into my heart."

Sometimes, getting to a point where one can say the prayer is difficult. However, once offered, the daily journey as a Christian begins. The prayer isn't a magic bullet or one-shot solution. The daily journey with the Lord is not always easy. In fact, in my experience, the difficulties in my life have strengthened my faith.

The beautiful part about this whole thing is that God always stands ready to count every hair on our heads, to care about everything that happens to us. Though I find it hard to believe at times, He'll never give me more than I can handle.

Someone once said to me that God is a gentleman and, as such, He'll never force His way into someone's life. He wants an invitation. He wants us to need Him and to cast our cares on Him. His love for us is totally beyond our comprehension.

Every day I ask God to walk with me and guide me, to do what He wants me to do, and live the way He wants me to live. Sometimes He gives me answers I don't want to hear. Sometimes He answers prayers with what I need rather than what I want. Amazingly, when I do what He says, things turn out better in the long run, despite any short-term unpleasantness I might experience.

I said my first prayer at thirteen. During my Confirmation service in the Presbyterian Church, when it came time to say that I was committing my life to Christ, I wanted to turn around and shout it to the congregation. Something welled up in me that I didn't totally understand at the time.

That evening, my older sister prayed with me to receive God into my heart. No great bells rang. No great light shot down from heaven to slay me, but I did see the path of my life before me. To this day, I am truly grateful to her for that very special prayer. Some may have vivid and earth-shaking experiences when they invite God into their lives. My experience came quietly, and it began the journey in which I listen for that still, small voice to guide me every day.

Thank you, Lord, for walking on this earth and dying for my sins, so that I can have eternal life. Thank you for putting people in my life who shared the message of Your grace. Thank you for all the great teachers You have sent to show me how to walk by faith, not by sight.

Day by Day

My life with the Lord remains a daily journey filled with prayer. The more I walk with Him, the deeper my respect and love for Him. When I cannot see the solution to a problem that feels like Mount Everest to me, He shows me that the problem is solvable, and that nothing is impossible with God.

Many times, God instructs me to do things that require a leap of faith. No matter what scary situation I encounter, I know He walks with me everywhere I go. He'll never let go of me, even if I let go of Him. In this time of continual and rapid change, He is truly the constant that I can always depend on. I may stray from the path He has for me, but He'll always be there to lead me back to His path so I can go where He wants me to go. He is my constant and patient guide.

I may not always stop what I'm doing to pray. Sometimes as I drive I'll chat with Him. He is so approachable. Unlike human friends who may hear our woes and make judgments, He listens and wraps His love around us like a warm, cuddly blanket.

Life hasn't always turned out as perfectly as I planned.

I never thought that fourteen years of marriage would end in divorce. Losing a job when business went sour for the bank I worked for wasn't part of my plan either.

As it turned out, the job I lost ultimately made me realize that I had not chosen the career that God wanted for me. Now I understand why the job I lost wasn't right for me.

Losing that job didn't make me less of a person, although at the time I felt really rotten about it. Ultimately, I realized that I had not chosen the profession best suited to my gifts and talents. No matter what I did in banking, I wouldn't flourish, and I knew I wouldn't reach God's calling there. Banking was a stepping stone though.

Now as a business owner, my experience as a banker has kept me out of trouble. My knowledge of business, what makes it work, and what makes it fail comes from helping other people finance their businesses.

Fortunately, God has walked with me day by day so I could deal with life's detours. He has such a better plan mapped out than I do. I'm lucky that God has such infinite patience and indulges my meanderings.

One day when in my mid-twenties, as I drove to a new place, I got lost and drove around a bit before I found my way again. I tried this little road, thinking it would take me in the right direction. When that didn't work, I tried a different one. Finally, I got so frustrated, I cried out, "Lord, help me! I don't know where I'm going!"

Sure enough, the next turn I took led me back to where I needed to be. I realized that the same thing happens when following the Lord. We may lose the path sometime, but

He's always there waiting for us. Like the highway I couldn't find, God always waits to place us back on the right path.

When the fog settles over the road so we can't see it clearly with our human vision, God may direct us to do something we don't fully understand. At times, we have to move out into the abyss armed with the shield of faith to follow this path. I've found that when I'm willing to take a risk in faith and obedience to Him, God honors the fact that I follow Him.

I Corinthians 13:12 says, "We see in a glass darkly, but then face to face…" On the other side of obedience and a step of faith that God has directed us to take, we can see clearly that God had a plan in mind all along.

Every person I meet on life's journey may have a profound influence on my life and play an integral part in my walk with God. Often I don't know how people and events will influence my life until much later. For example, at one consulting firm I worked for, a brilliant consultant mentored me and taught me how to develop training programs. What I learned from him has helped me immensely in the work I do now.

Day by day, God gives me just a little more insight, a little more light on the path, a bigger picture of where He wants me. If He gave too much insight into my ultimate path with Him, I might jump in there and mess things up. He really doesn't need my help planning things!

Fortunately, God takes me by the hand every day and ever so patiently guides my every step. I'm like the child who has just learned to walk. The child takes a few steps, then a few more, then goes too fast and topples to the floor. His parent patiently picks him up and helps him get going again. I don't always pay attention to God's guidance, and sometimes I go too fast, but He still waits patiently and quietly to lead me on again.

Thank you, Lord, for taking my hand and walking with me every day, and for the people you place in my path on life's road. Your patience with my wanderings and humanness just demonstrates Your unfaltering grace.

The Frenetic Pace

I went to a retreat one weekend where the retreat leader said, "The key to prayer is not so much talking as listening." He also said that we need to learn how to "be" rather than "do." What a simple but powerful message. We so easily give God our "to do" list for Him, when maybe we should hear His "to do" list for us.

On the Monday morning after that retreat, I woke up in my usual frenetic pace and found myself "giving" my morning prayers to God and doing all the talking. Then I stopped and asked God how He wanted me to start my day. He told me simply to do less busy work and give the children fewer instructions.

For once in my life I relaxed during the morning routine with my three daughters. The morning seemed much less stressful. The unmade beds, yesterday's clothes piled on the floor, and all the girlie stuff lying around the bathroom counter didn't bother me.

God also reminded me to observe and listen to my children's needs by watching them. I learned so much by watching and listening to them, and I realized that they just needed me to let them be themselves and sometimes help them less.

The morning that God told me to slow down, my oldest daughter tiptoed into the laundry room to iron her school uniform before school. Instead of complaining because she hadn't put the skirt in the wash early enough so that it got ironed on ironing day, I didn't say anything. I just let her iron away, which worked fine for her. I'm sure my children felt relief that God told me to cool it.

I'm learning to talk less and listen more. Not only do the children need me to talk less, listen more, and really hear them, but most people in my life probably prefer that. When I envision Jesus among his disciples, I don't see him talking incessantly and giving instructions. Rather, I see Him observing, listening, teaching the disciples based on what they say, what He observed in the world, and what He observed them doing and thinking. As a Christian, if I strive to imitate Christ, then I must be quiet, observant and patient with my responses to people and events. The quiet allows me to reflect, to come to more complete conclusions about life and all that it includes.

Spending the weekend at a retreat in the Texas Hill Country helped me to practice quietness and observation. It gave me a chance to "be" instead of "do," to listen instead of talk, to stop and notice God's wonderful creation.

So often, trying to keep up with three children, a consulting business, and a household gets in the way of asking God, "What do you want me to do?" My challenge lies in stopping to be with God and hear His call for daily life, instead of racing around the city at a frenetic pace. Daily, I must continue to stop and reflect in a world that moves at break-neck speed and expects me to move at its frenetic pace.

Forgive me, Lord, for running around too fast and forgetting that I'm here to serve You. Remind me when I'm running too fast to stop and seek Your guidance. Make me more reflective about You, Your holy word, and Your path for me.

Way Too Proud

Oh, I am so able. I'm tough. I can make it. I remember, right after I divorced, telling a psychologist that I was one *tough hombre*.

I find myself now totally humbled at God's feet. In my weakness, He is strong. In my infirmity, He is the healer. When I am quiet and heed His call, my actions result in power; not because of me, but because of Him.

Perhaps others feel as I do. We must perform or show our friends, siblings or parents that we can handle anything. We must be perfect. We need to have everything together, with lots of money in a retirement fund, plenty of insurance, and no worries. Yet God doesn't require that we have everything perfectly worked out. He understands our daily frustrations better than we do sometimes. We have set up an expectation for what we need to do to be okay. In God's eyes we are okay exactly as we are.

Because I am *so* imperfect and perfectly human, God can be perfect. When I don't cover up my shortcomings, God stands strong. Sometimes my pride gets in the way of asking people to help me.

A friend gave me a new perspective on asking people

for help. He said, "When you don't ask people for help, you rob them of an opportunity to feel good." Then he asked, "Don't you feel good when you help people?"

I realized that he was right. I worried so much about proving to people that I could handle things, that I forgot how they might feel helping someone.

You know, we can even learn a lot from our dogs. I had a Rosie. As she got older, she found it harder and harder to climb the stairs to be near me and my daughters. She never worried about getting older and her inability to run the stairs, as I might. She just contentedly and slowly climbed the stairs to spend time with the people she loved. Pride never got in her way.

I have a friend whose wife divorced him. Then nine months later, he lost his very best friend in a tragic accident. He told me that every Sunday when he went to church, he couldn't help but cry about losing his friend. About six months after his friend died, he could finally go to church without sobbing, a great achievement for him. How dear that he could admit that he found losing his marriage and his friend so close together too hard to bear.

My friend's story helped me to realize that it's okay to admit the depth of our pain. We really don't have to have it together all the time. I admire this man very much because he can explain his profound reaction to the loss of a dear life-long friend while he celebrates his friend's life.

Once he planned to celebrate his deceased friend's birthday and some of his friends found this strange. I marveled at the thoughtfulness. I saw the celebration of the birthday of a lost friend as a true way of dealing with a loss.

God has helped me to realize that I don't need to be strong all of the time and that sometimes my pride really gets in the way.

Thank you, God, for showing me my pride. Help me to remember that my weakness allows You to be strong. Help me to learn how to accept help from people.

Letting Go

One of the hardest lessons I've had to learn as a Christian is how to let go of anger and hurt and to forgive people. After all, those feelings, like baggage, do nothing but weigh me down. God doesn't say to forgive when I feel like it or when I get around to it. He commands me to always forgive others.

When I forgive someone, I benefit so much by letting go of that weight, the baggage that's dragging me down. Harboring ugly feelings or old hurts can make us physically ill. God means for us to have clean hearts that don't hold on to anger and hurt. He can heal our hearts and help them grow so we can have fresh new love and life.

Forgiveness doesn't mean acting as if nothing has happened and avoiding a person or situation. Forgiveness creates reconciliation among all concerned. The more forgiving I do, the easier it becomes. Sometimes I have to make myself pray for people I need to forgive, and God always blesses me through these prayers. I really benefit more than anyone else, because I hurt myself if I don't forgive someone. Letting go also means not always fixing everything.

Recently, I went to a convention where I came across two women in unrelated instances. Both projected on to me their reaction to a particular situation of mine. Based on their own reality, they assumed I felt the way they would about the situation. In both instances, I finally said that I thought we had to agree to disagree, rather than try to convince each other of the validity of the other one's viewpoint.

Several days after I left the convention, I thought I should write each of them a note to express my admiration for them and appreciation for their friendship. However, for some reason, I felt God didn't want me to do that.

I thought about it and when I asked God about it, He replied that I should wait and when they needed me, they'd contact me. And I realized that I had to let go of the fact that they might still be thinking that I was devastated by my current situation, even though I neither thought nor communicated that. I continued to pray about this, and God continued to confirm that I shouldn't try to fix this situation. Ultimately, I realized my whole need to write these notes to the women came from my pride. Deep down I wanted to prove that I was handling the situation just fine.

It wasn't my responsibility to make them change their minds or fix the situation. I just needed to let go and let God handle it.

Once again, I needed to let go of the reins and let God handle things. After all, He did create the universe. I think He can handle misunderstandings among friends. Letting go sometimes means letting someone else take care of you.

One time I had to go out of town and a friend kindly

volunteered to take care of my dog. As I gave him instructions about caring for the dog, I remember telling him that I was running out of dog food and needed to get that before I left. He called back awhile later and said he'd try to get the dog food for me.

"Oh, you don't have to do that," I said. And I remember thinking I didn't want to impose on him.

After a few seconds on the phone, he said almost apologetically, "Oh, okay, I won't."

I found it so hard to let go of taking care of everything that I couldn't even let a friend help out when he really wanted to help. I'm beginning to realize that often people do want to help in any way that they can. And I'd do the same for my friend and never think twice about it.

In a way, I responded coldly to my friend. God shows me daily how He sends people to help me along life's way, and if I deny their help, then in a way, I'm denying God's help.

When my children first learned to drive, one of my biggest challenges was letting go of the fear that I would lose one in a terrible car accident. When my oldest daughter had been driving on her own for almost a year, she had the opportunity to visit her cousin, who lives in a small town about 45 minutes away.

I had to decide whether to let her drive on the highway, by herself, with all those other insane drivers. She had been coached by a driving instructor and her dad on the freeway, but I hadn't coached her driving on the freeway.

My fear of her emotional reaction to my coaching while driving seventy miles an hour kept me from spending some time driving with her on the freeway.

When she had the opportunity to visit her cousin, I had lots of logical reasons why she shouldn't. I prayed about this and felt God told me that I should let her go by herself. I realized I needed to trust God to take care of my child. The hardest thing to realize was that if something did happen to her on the highway, she'd go safely home to the arms of her heavenly Father.

I could do nothing to stop something like that and saw this as the ultimate point of letting go for me. For she really is God's child, I'm only her caretaker on this earth. She truly belongs to God, a hard but important realization, so I have to let go of her.

Many times I have trouble letting go of something I have done against God. Psalms says that God forgives our sins and removes them from us as far as the east is from the west. The Lord totally forgets our sins when He forgives us. Sometimes we find total forgiveness hard to accept. When I have repeatedly asked God to forgive me for something, and He answers saying He has already forgotten my sin, I realize that I'm the one who needs to let go of it. He doesn't even remember that it happened.

Thank you, Lord, for helping me let go and trust You more. Please show me where my worry gets in the way of faith. Help me to surrender control to You. Strengthen my peace of knowing that You are ultimately in control of my life.

Rejoice in the Lord Always

One day as I was walking and trying to think of positive things about my life, I kept thinking of negative things, stuff that made me angry, things that were wrong with my life. The Lord gave me a gift by reminding me that He didn't say to rejoice in Him when things are rosy. He said to rejoice in Him always!

So I reviewed each item on my mental "what's wrong" list and thanked God for it. Amazingly, I felt truly joyful inside, as though someone had lifted the weight of the world from my shoulders. He lifted that weight and showed me, just as the Apostle Paul wrote in Philippians, "Rejoice in the Lord always, and again I say rejoice." What a better approach to life.

Sometimes rejoicing may start with, "I don't like this, Lord, but I thank You and rejoice in You anyway, because You have commanded me to."

I have to admit that I don't always find rejoicing in Him easy, it's just better than moaning about what's wrong. Rejoicing uplifts me, thankfulness keeps me in the right frame of mind and builds a grateful heart in me. Joy helps me find the opportunity in situations rather than the stumbling blocks.

God doesn't need an explanation for my gratitude for something I don't like. He knows my heart better than I do. He knows my intent better than I do. I believe He honors honest acceptance of unpleasant events. How wonderful to have a Father in heaven from whom we don't need to hide anything for fear of disapproval. We can't hide things from Him, because He knows us better than we know ourselves.

The unpleasant events in life act like fertilizer. Fertilizer smells bad and too much of it will burn the grass, but just enough makes the grass thick and green. Unpleasant events in our lives don't always smell so good, and when they happen, they burn, but in the long run they enrich us.

One time I lost a job and that really did burn, because I pride myself in always making things work and performing as the ultimate professional. When I lost the job, I thought of it as the worst thing that could happen to me. Not only did it hurt my pride, but it created incredible financial burdens for our family. Now, looking back more than twenty years later, I see losing that job as a blessing. If I hadn't lost my job, I might have still forged through in a career that I didn't really enjoy. That situation helped me grow as a professional and a Christian. Now I work in a profession where I feel God can use me the most.

Losing the job was like spreading fertilizer on the lawn, and it made my life so much richer. Setbacks like this one seem to work to make me stronger and wiser. The growth prepares me for some unforeseen bumps in life's road. Sometimes overcoming a setback will help me help someone else going through this same thing. I know God will never give me more than I can handle, even when I don't have enough faith in myself to think I can handle what happens.

Setbacks remind me of the process used to refine precious metals referred to in Malachi 3:2-3 where it says the metal smith's fire makes us shine like newly-smelted and polished gold.

Thank you, Lord, for everything, both good and bad. Help me to remember to thank You for everything, even the stuff I don't like.

All Good Things Come from Thee, Oh Lord

Every good thing bestowed and every perfect gift is from above, coming down from the Father of lights, with whom there is no variation, or shifting shadow.
James 1:17

God calls us to act as good stewards of His resources. I find it so easy to think my resources belong to me rather than to the Lord. Yes, I may work hard to earn money, but God has given me talents, gifts, and abilities, and blesses my business daily. We have an obligation to use our gifts to glorify Him and all our resources together are His, whether we like to admit it or not.

I once heard a speaker/singer talk about how he went to a singing audition without focusing on glorifying God, and he failed. That night he promised God that he'd never again use his voice for anything but to glorify God. God has blessed this man so much, and the man has shared his gifts and talents with other speakers to help them grow.

Yes, I'm proud of my accomplishments. Yet if it

weren't for God's continuing encouragement, I might have given up on my company years ago. So many times I doubted that the firm could succeed, but He knew so much more than I did. Many times God has literally guided me through a business relationship.

At one point, I was truly ready to give up the business and take a corporate job, but God encouraged me to hang in there. Sticking with my business has helped my faith grow so much more than any corporate job. My consulting business allows me to use my gifts and talents to help companies achieve more and it allows me to share God's love, even if I never say anything about God. God has not made me very astute or patient in handling corporate politics, so having my own consulting firm makes better use of my gifts, skills and energy.

Children, one of our most precious gifts from God, truly belong to Him, and that is one of the hardest issues I have had to deal with in the last few years. Many times when my children leave my sphere of influence, I remind myself that I must release them to God.

When they were home, every time all three of them drove off to school in the little red car, I had to let go and visualize God's angels around the car. As hard as I find it to comprehend, I know God loves my children more than I do. The more I can let my children grow and mature in their lives and their faith in God, the better. God expects me to guide them and nurture their faith without trying to control everything. Frankly, they learn a lot from my life example—that God will always take care of us and our needs. I must share with them how God has worked in my life when I trust Him.

God has entrusted me with these children and their faith while on earth. I have a responsibility to live up to the task. They will glean more from my actions than my words. I must demonstrate how to walk in an often unspiritual world with God at my side to guide me. I encourage them to use their special gifts, to help them realize how special and unique they are because God especially crafted each of them with His own hands.

Thank you, Lord, for the resources You have provided for me and my precious children. Thank you for Your wisdom to provide for us what we need in spite of what we want. Thank you for Your rich and precious gifts. Help me to always remember that all resources come from You. Make me a wise steward of Your resources.

Talents and Gifts

God doesn't casually request that we use our talents and gifts. He commands us to use them. Recently, I observed a very gifted retreat leader set the tone for the retreat as contemplative, not by saying, "This retreat is contemplative," but by the way he opened the session, introduced his wife, and led the opening prayer.

He never focused on himself. Instead, he focused on those who had traveled from far away to attend the retreat. Each time we returned from a break, the leader gave suggestions about books that he had read. His wife, equally gifted, introduced the staff that served us during the retreat. Her loving manner encouraged the staff members to introduce themselves without feeling awkward. She helped set the tone for the community of people at the retreat during the entire weekend. God's glow radiated from her face every time I talked to her. She stopped and noticed people individually for their contributions to small group discussions and other activities. She emanated the beauty and peace of Christ through her soft voice and kind eyes.

At the same retreat, I met a gifted tennis coach who said that his ministry was teaching people to play tennis.

He demonstrated how God coaches us. He worked with three of us at once and gave very specific corrections on how to improve our strokes. He let us play games on the court to improve our consistency in hitting the ball, and he didn't give us lessons that we couldn't use.

He always commented on what we performed correctly. If any of us started fussing at ourselves about what we did wrong, he pointed out something right about what we did. This man, an incredibly accomplished tennis player, treated us like the most gifted and talented tennis players in the world. He spoke to us kindly, yet deliberately. Just learning tennis from him, I felt the love and acceptance of Jesus.

I heard a woman speak who teaches critically ill children in hospitals. In the talk, she recounted story after story of young children with whom she built a bond, taught, and often nurtured until their last moments of life. She shared many things that caused many of us in the audience to comment about how we could not possibly do her job, since it was so apparent that God had literally appointed this woman to carry out a very unique ministry to some very precious and special children. God had given her whatever patience, understanding or nurturing ability she needed to perform this job.

One of my sisters had an art school where she inspired and guided the minds, hearts and creativity of children. A gifted educator, she has a pragmatic way with children that provides them with evenness, a real bonus to the cool art instruction she gives the children. In a job she had before opening her art school, she used her musical, artistic and teaching gifts to mold young children. She didn't study education for years and years to learn how to inspire children. God gave her a very special gift for that.

While in high school, one of my nephews discovered his gift for running. A true natural, and as fast as the wind, he rose to stardom in his very first year in track. When he attended the Junior Olympics, he ranked thirteenth in the nation. When only in the eighth grade, the high school track coach proclaimed him faster than anyone on the high school team. My nephew didn't boast about his accomplishments, he just quietly won race after race.

My parents, both trained counselors and gifted grandparents, blessed our whole family with their very giving attitude. The accomplishments of their children and grandchildren pleased them so much. They never forgot anyone's birthday and almost always brought back trinkets and gifts from their many trips. God gave them both certain wisdom and gifts in counseling children and grandchildren. My parents counseled my children and me through some of our very rough times.

I find it a wonderful blessing to observe people and see how God bestows gifts and talents. The most joyful and productive people in the world are those who use their special gifts and talents. True fulfillment in life comes from following God and using what He has given us.

Thank you, Lord, for the richness of Your gifts. Help me to use my gifts in the way that you want me to. Guide me so that I may help others discover the special gifts you have given them.

A Prayerful Life

I heard my pastor say, "If each of us prays for ten people a day, imagine the lives that God will touch."

What an opportunity to enrich the lives of others and share the wonder of God. God so richly blesses me when I pray for others, and it keeps me close to God. In a Sunday school class on prayer, I learned to pray using ACTS: A for adoration, C for confession, T for thanksgiving and S for supplication.

Adoration means admiring God simply because He is Almighty God and praising Him for His awe and splendor. He doesn't need us to fight His battles for Him, even though we often try. He deserves our adoration and praise. In adoration, we praise and recognize God for being God.

Though almighty and incomprehensible, He's not a policeman with a big night stick. He can do what He wants, but He chose to give up His own son so we could have eternal life. I know I couldn't do that for someone else.

I look at the earth, a miniscule part of the universe, down to the tiny ant that makes a home in my grass, and I stand amazed that the same God who created both of these looks upon me as His child. Adoration simply says, "You are great. You are wonderful. You are the one almighty God."

In confession, I admit to God how I've gone against Him by the things I've done, or left undone. This goes beyond following principles laid out in the Bible or shared by our pastors. If God directs us to do something and we don't…we have sinned against Him. And He always directs us to do things for our own good. God forgives my sins totally, a lot better than I forgive myself. He doesn't keep score or put me on probation. He forgets the sin and allows me to move forward.

Confession cleanses the heart and the soul and reminds us of God's gift of grace. His ultimate act of grace was giving His son so we can live eternally with God someday. Remembering that sacrifice reminds me of God's great forgiveness. As it says in Psalms 103:12, He removes my sin as far as the east is from the west. That doesn't make me want to go against God to see what I can get away with. In fact, it humbles me to seek His guidance even more. It also reminds me not to judge others, because I'm just as imperfect as my neighbor.

A prayer of thanksgiving shows my gratitude to God for all things He sends my way, both good and bad. I have to admit that sometimes I don't feel thankful and it's really hard to do.

I believe everything happens for a reason and the more I thank Him for everything that happens, the more joy and contentment I experience. Constant thankfulness will grow grateful hearts. We receive great graces from thanking God even when we don't feel thankful. Thanking God when I'm having a bad day is a lot harder than thanking God when things go right. I view the tough times as gifts to help me grow. In Malachi 3:2, it says the refiner's fire in the tough times just makes us into purer silver for the Lord. The tough times also enable me to help other people who experience the same trials I do.

In the last few years I've had plenty of opportunities to hear about the tough times of another single parent. My own difficult times meant I could say, "You're right. You're dealing with a tough situation similar to one I experienced, and God stands right beside you to bring you through it. I know it isn't easy." The imperfectness of my life has helped these people more than anything else. I'm more help to them because I can share stories that demonstrate how God has helped me through a similar time.

The final part of ACTS is supplication, when we make requests of God. In order to track whom I need to pray for, I have a prayer list tacked on the bulletin board near my desk. During the day, I stop and review the list and ask God to answer each prayer for each person on the list.

God doesn't always answer my supplications in the way I want or expect, but He answers every prayer in some way. The more I pray for others in my supplications, the closer I stay to God. I find such blessings when I pray for others because it keeps me in constant communication with Him.

Some have asked me why I petition God for things when He knows what I want or need better than I know. I believe that God cherishes and wants a relationship with every person on earth. He blesses us by giving us the opportunity to ask for things in order to help strengthen our relationship with Him. Even though we often fall short in our covenant with Him, He still loves us and wishes to bless us and share His abundance with us.

Prayer is such a great way to strengthen our relationship with a loving, heavenly Father. He wants us to communicate with Him in the same way that earthly parents want our children to communicate with us.

Sometimes I feel that God wants me to pray for certain people or events. I try not to question, but to follow in faith. One time I felt led to pray for a friend whom I had not seen in about eight months. A couple of hours later his sister called me and told me that he and two of his children had been in a terrible car accident. Later that afternoon, as I prayed for his daughter who was in the back seat without a seat belt, God gave me a vision of Jesus standing over the console of the Suburban holding the sides out, protecting my friend and his son. Even though the Suburban flipped over five times, all three of them walked away with minor injuries!

Any time I recount this story, I can't help but weep. Not because I did something so fantastic, but because God gave me a message and I acted on it, then God revealed the power of following His lead. I thank God for saving the lives of my precious friends.

A prayerful life requires quiet time to listen to God. He constantly speaks with us. We have only to pay attention, quietly, and thoughtfully.

With the busy lives that we lead, finding quiet time to

hear God challenges us all. That fast pace of the world makes stopping and listening to God very difficult, yet we must stop and listen to Him in order to carry out the plans He has for us.

I adore You, Father, for the beautiful creation of the earth that You have made for us. I confess that I do not always do as You ask. Thank you, Lord, for giving me the structure of the ACTS for prayer. Help me, Lord, to hear you when your Holy Spirit bids me to pray for someone. Even if I don't know why, help me to step out in faith and pray for the person. Please walk with me always and help me to remember You in everything I do.

Thank you, Lord, for teaching me that prayerfulness means staying quiet. Thank you, Lord, for the opportunity to pray for others. The more I pray for them, the more I am blessed. Thank you for those times of quiet and solitude, when I can just listen and hear Your still, small voice. The more prayerful I am, the more peaceful my life. Help me to remember to slow down the frenetic pace, to reflect, to live a mindful and prayerful life.

Dreams and Visions

And it will come about after this that I will pour out My Spirit on all mankind; And your sons and daughters with prophesy, Your old men will dream dreams, Your young men will see visions.

Joel 2:28

God sends fascinating messages through dreams. They don't come to all people like a prediction from a crystal ball, but more a way of the Father communicating something to us that will give us assurance, direction or information that we cannot otherwise see. I always look at dreams as a way for God to communicate with me. I always ask Him if a dream had a message. I've tried to help my children see how God speaks to them through their dreams, too.

While praying about moving from Dallas to San Antonio, I had a dream that my children and I were driving down Military Highway through Camp Bullis to the children's school. As we looked for a house for us to live in, I found a newly listed rental property that fit our needs and budget. I interpreted that dream as confirmation from

God that I should indeed move to that city.

When we moved to San Antonio and were driving to school one day, I noticed something. We were driving down Military Highway through Camp Bullis to get to TMI, the children's school! That really showed me that I had followed God's lead by moving to San Antonio.

Once at a retreat, the leader asked us to read a chapter of Henri Nouwen's book, *Becoming the Beloved.* I read the chapter right before I went to sleep. That night I had a dream that showed me how to become God's beloved. In the dream, I found myself sitting in a meeting of some kind. Someone sitting behind me put his arms around me and I felt the warm comfort engulf my being. Then another person hugged me and I had the same feeling. Somehow, I knew these people loved me unconditionally, including all my faults and shortcomings. God gave me this dream to say that to become His beloved, I only need to let Him love me for my complete self, including my imperfections.

God gives us dreams and visions that He knows will mean something to us and will give us only as much information as we can handle. I believe that is why God gives us only part of the picture sometimes. If He told us the whole story in advance, we might get in His way.

Thank you, Lord, for enlightening and blessing me with dreams and helping me to see that You love my faults as much as my strengths. Thank you for Your guidance and assurance through dreams.

Spiritual Battles

My pastor once said that sometimes we fight our spiritual battles with human logic, which is bound to fail. I like to think that I have control of everything and that I can get through anything by figuring it out. But logically, why should I do that? If my Father in heaven knows so much more and is so much more powerful than I, how logical is it to think that I can figure it out better than He can?

When faced with troubles, we need to utilize prayer, a shining sword, the most powerful weapon in our arsenal. Many of our trials and tribulations come to us through Satan, and we often choose to battle him directly instead of using our mightiest weapon. God is so much more competent to fight our spiritual battles, yet we think we have to battle it out alone. I know He doesn't want to leave us out in the cold alone. I also think He expects us to ask for His help when we need it.

Satan doesn't present himself in a red suit with red glowing eyes and horns. More clever than that, he plays with our inherent fears or tendency to worry. Sometimes he even uses unsuspecting people to work against us.

When I heard the pastor make his comment about

fighting spiritual wars, I realized that I had spent the last four months doing just that. I had moved to a new town and immediately wallowed in human worry and fear.

How will I develop business in a new town? How will I manage with the children's father in a different town? How will I make new friends like the ones I had for years in another town? How can I ever buy a house in the new town?

Many of these questions got in the way of moving forward and trusting God. When my pastor talked about fighting spiritual battles, I suddenly realized that I had forgotten to fight spiritual battles with a spiritual weapon! I felt as though I had gone to a pistol duel with a water gun. I didn't stop worrying overnight, but I started turning things over to God, one by one. I came to realize that Satan can sometimes twist something in our minds so that we end up worrying about something ridiculous.

The best prayer I can use against Satan is offering praise to God. Sometimes I even think playing music that praises God creates an atmosphere filled with God's spirit. Praising God keeps me focused on lifting my heart toward the Lord rather than groveling in the dirt and looking around at what I need to worry about.

Ephesians 6:12 tells us, "For our struggle is not against flesh and blood, but against the rulers, against the principalities of darkness in the heavenly places." If you can remember that, the next time you argue or disagree with someone, ask God to take over the conversation. Expect Him to take charge of the communication between you, so that those forces of darkness don't enter in. People can come against you because of these spirits of darkness and never even realize they're doing it.

Sometimes, even in a conversation with a friend, I can see that a friend's commitment to Christ affects how well I communicate or how accepted I feel, no matter what I say. God's spirit in those people gives me strength to fight the spiritual battles.

Thank you, Lord, for sending me to the church to hear the pastor who reminded me to fight my spiritual battles with the most powerful and best weapon possible—prayer.

Follow Him

Following God's lead can prove challenging. In my experience, it takes lots of practice, especially when following Him means making a sacrifice or doing something that seems illogical.

In the late 90s, God called me to make a move from one town to another. My immediate response was, "Are you crazy? How am I going to do that?"

I appointed two prayer warriors to help me seek God's guidance about the move. He confirmed through one of these women that I should move. Once I got to the new town with my three daughters, my business suffered terribly. I even sometimes looked skyward and asked, "Lord, did I hear You right?"

The ultimate lesson I learned about following God is that He may lead us through trials. Following Him does not mean things will be easy and rosy. Look at the Apostle Paul.

For Paul, following the Lord meant being thrown in jail. Yet Paul never lost heart about his situation. In Philippians he says, "Not that I speak from want, for I have learned to be content in whatever circumstances I am." God took care of Paul. One time God caused an earthquake so that Paul could escape prison!

When we take care of His business, He'll take care of ours. When we follow His lead, He will take care of our needs. Sometimes we may have to pray for faith to follow Him, and following His lead really takes practice.

So many well-meaning people want to give advice. I went to a conference recently and received lots of advice and differing opinions about how to grow as a professional speaker. On the last day, as I engaged in a conversation with a gentleman, I realized that I really needed to listen only to my instincts to know what is really right for me to do, especially since I have God to guide me. The man confirmed that people will give us gobs of good advice, some that we can use and some that we can't, but we can't use all of it.

I can learn so much from people who have stubbed their toes, then picked themselves up and moved forward. I relish the counsel of those who have been where I am now. The key is to measure advice against my goals, what I know about myself and where I think God is leading me.

Dear Lord,

I make the simple so difficult. When I hear You telling me to do something, I should do it without question. You have proven so many times that You have it figured out much better than I ever could. In fact, I know You cannot reveal too much to me at a time or I will mess things up by getting in the way.

So many times You have told me to do something and I

didn't. In some cases, I didn't do what you said for years! You are patient, Lord, and it's a good thing. Otherwise, You would have given up on me a long time ago!

Following You can be such a test of faith. Sometimes what You tell me to do is probably very illogical in the eyes of the world. I guess some things You say should be illogical to human minds, since we are so finite and You are so infinite. Sometimes people will ask me why You allow tragedies to happen, like a child dying or a drastic natural disaster. And my answer is that You are God, and infinite, therefore far beyond our human comprehension. We cannot know or understand everything You have in Your plan.

Please help me, Lord, to follow You every day and to accept whatever You have for me.

Faith

Look at the birds of the air, that they do not sow, neither do they reap, nor gather into barns, and yet your heavenly Father feeds them. Are you not worth much more than they? And which of you by being anxious can add a single cubit to his life's span? And why are you anxious about clothing? Observe how the lilies of the field grow, they do not toil nor do they spin. Yet I say to you that even Solomon in all his glory did not clothe himself like one of these.

But if God so arrays the grass of the field which is alive today and tomorrow is thrown into the furnace, will He not much more do so for you, O men of little faith?

Matthew 6:26-30

The message from this passage in Matthew is easier to hear than to put into practice. Time and time again the Lord has demonstrated His care for even the finest and smallest details of my life, yet I still choose to worry and give in to anxiety. When I put my faith in Him, I must let go of control and know that He has a bigger plan than I can see or even begin to comprehend.

In the late fall of 1996, one-and-a-half years after I started my consulting practice, I seriously considered taking a corporate job. I felt that God kept saying that I shouldn't worry because there were things about the business that I couldn't see. This message from Him continued for about five months and I almost gave up.

One April day, on a Sunday afternoon, I felt God saying that things would change the next day. At 4:30 p.m. on Monday, I received three calls in a row requesting my consulting services. He so faithfully provides for every need, even when I don't believe it. Each time I have to really trust God for a need, my faith grows a little stronger.

God's logic doesn't always align with ours, but He knows more than we do. I remember that I once wrote a proposal for consulting services for a potential client. I drew up the proposal and thought about the fees. I came up with a number and entered it into the proposal. I felt God saying the fee wasn't high enough.

So I started arguing with Him. "Gee, Lord, what if it's too much and they don't hire me? You know my situation. I have three kids to feed. I *need* this work."

God won the argument, and I put a higher dollar amount on the proposal. In faith, I followed what I felt that God had directed me to do. I presented this proposal to the potential client. She looked through it quickly and went to the back to see the dollar amount for the contract and exclaimed, "This is cheap!"

God is even a great businessman. He knows the value of my work better than I do. He also knew that the work I had proposed would take much longer than I had anticipated, so the higher price was more appropriate. This client ended up sending me more work after the first project. God helped me create a strong relationship with the client, so that the client felt very comfortable paying me for my services.

Thank you, Lord, for the gift of faith. Thanks for guiding me along, ever so gently, through life's events, like the moonlight filtering through tall forest trees. Help me to hear and trust You more. Help me to use the gift of faith better.

His Eye Is On the Sparrow

Dear Lord,

The song "His Eye Is On the Sparrow" asks, "Why should I be discouraged? Why should the shadows come?...When Jesus is my portion, a constant friend is He. His eye is on the sparrow and I know he watches me."

I have trouble listening to this song without weeping, maybe because sometimes I feel like a sparrow, small and unimportant. Yet, as a sparrow, I am more likely to depend on You. Almighty God, Your power overwhelms me, yet at the same time You care for my smallest, most insignificant needs. You demonstrate time and time again that You will provide for the smallest detail in my life. Thank you for always being there. Help me to walk forward in life, in faith, knowing that You watch over me as my constant friend.

Miracles

The miracle is in the belief.
                    Johnnye Jean Lovett, 7-30-96

One day in a telephone conversation with my mother about how God had answered some prayers, I told her that the way something happened might seem like a coincidence to some, but that I felt God had a hand in the situation.

She replied, "The miracle is in the belief."

When I marveled at the profound nature of the statement, she acted as if she wasn't even sure why she had said it, as though God literally spoke through her. What a blessing to have a mother so in tune with God.

She's right. We can probably explain away miracles in many cases. But to those who believe that God has a definite hand in their lives, miracles happen daily, even hourly.

I recall a time when my consulting firm experienced a tight cash flow situation. A client had indicated that he needed about $8,000 of work in August, and then at the last minute changed plans. I couldn't rebook the time with a different client, and that caused the cash flow crunch. I needed to pay my rent and didn't have quite enough money for it.

I felt God telling me not to worry about the money. He would provide. I prayed for accounts payable clerks at all the companies where I had outstanding invoices, that they pay my invoices quickly. I thought of all kinds of things I could do, but I trusted in God. Following God's lead, I paid my rent on Friday, knowing that I had at least until Monday to make sure my account had enough money it.

On Saturday I received a notice in the mail that income from a farm that I owned with my siblings was being direct-deposited into my account and would be available on Monday. The amount was at least double that few hundred dollars that I needed. Although some people would call this a coincidence, I feel that God had His hand in this true miracle.

Things like this happen every day, and I think God wants us to trust that He will not forsake us. He will always provide for our needs, even though sometimes we think He doesn't hear us. He is truly our Jehovah Jireh, our provider. As God provided for the Israelites in freeing them from bondage in Egypt, He does the same for us. I don't suggest that people go around writing checks they can't cover, but I do know when God gives a specific direction like He gave me, He knows something that I don't.

God doesn't always answer our prayers the way we want Him to. Sometimes He gives us what we need rather than what we want. He always hears our prayers and responds to them with His best answer. He is a very generous God.

Truly, miracles happen every day, and we only notice them when we open our hearts to God's power. What miracles has God put in your life? Watch for them. Open your eyes to the miracles God gives you every day.

Please, Lord, give us the faith and awareness to see Your miracles that happen around us every day. Give us the gift of faith to believe that You will always provide for our every need.

When I Survey the Wondrous Cross

The message of the cross truly humbles me. For my sake, God became a human and walked the earth. He allowed His death on a cross and experienced excruciating agony for me. The beauty of what God did for me truly awes me.

His act reminds me not to be boastful or self-centered, but rather, to focus on Him. When I have quiet time with the Lord, I stop and reflect on God and His power. Rather than focusing on what I can do or on my next task, I have time to contemplate on our gracious God and His amazing love. I can bring petitions to Him and know that He will answer them. I know that He sees us in our everyday lives and has mercy on us.

Jesus demonstrated the ultimate mercy. He silently hung in pain on the cross so we, who turn our backs on God, could live eternally in heaven with Him. He loved us so much that He endured not just death, but excruciating death. After carrying the cross of His death up a long, dusty road like a criminal, the Roman soldiers drove nails through his hands and feet. He hung there until He gave His very life so that we could have abundant life. His humility surpasses any human being on the planet. We cannot comprehend the humility of our Father in heaven.

When we drown ourselves in sin, He picks us up and gives us the opportunity for rebirth.

One day as I sat by a swimming pool writing, the man cleaning the pool fished out a beautiful moth that lay motionless on the surface. He said that these particular moths often dove into the pool and fluttered around until they drowned.

Rather than throw the moth in the grass, he gently lifted it out of the pool with his net and set it gently down to dry. I watched the insect. Its wings started to dry, then it crawled a few steps until finally it flew away.

This episode reminded me of how God pulls us out when we are drowning in sin. He doesn't just give up on us and toss us aside. He gently lifts us out of the mire and coddles us as we crawl along until we can fly. He gives us the great gift to life again and again.

Help me, dear Lord, to think of You on the cross, to remember that the victory for any battle I have or will have is already won. The blood You shed on Calvary is all we need to conquer any challenge. I am humbled, Lord, by Your amazing grace.

The Purity of Humility

I have come to realize that God doesn't treasure what I have accomplished as much as the world does. Rather, God cherishes my humility. He appreciates my willingness to be a fool for Him and to do what I think He wants me to do in spite of what might seem reasonable. When I start to pat myself on the back, God sometimes reminds me that He is the source of all I have.

Sometimes I get caught up in my achievements or in what I can do and I forget to give Him credit. If it weren't for God, I'd have never had the courage to start my own business, and I'd have never had the courage to follow some of the directions that God has given me. God doesn't care about the net income of my business. And while I believe divorce saddens Him, God does not condemn me for not succeeding in my marriage of fourteen years. God cares that I serve Him and do what He asks me to do. He has more concern that I trust Him in everything and honor Him.

Once, on a recent trip to San Francisco I misplaced my wallet. At first I felt very frustrated with myself for doing something so stupid, but then decided to make the most of it and be thankful that I could cancel the credit card and ATM card in my wallet. I asked God to handle the situation and He did. A San Franciscan cab driver discovered my wallet and called my office in San Antonio three times the day he found my wallet, because he wanted to get it back to me.

I don't think God said, "You dummy, how could you lose your wallet?" Instead, I think God said, "You have much to manage and think about. I want you to know that I care about every detail of your life. If you lose your wallet, people will send it back to you at their own inconvenience."

When I spoke to the cab driver who had my wallet, I asked him to take some money out of the wallet for his trouble and he refused. God's mercy and kindness and the kindness of the stranger in a city two time zones away overwhelm me.

So great, so kind, so generous, God ministers to our humility and our shortcomings. He holds us close to His heart and above all, desires that we follow Him. In our human frailty, we often forget Him, so from time to time He reminds us that no matter how dark or bad things look, He stands ready to care for us.

He demonstrated the ultimate humility to us by hanging on the cross like a common thief because He loved us.

Thank you, Lord, for reminding me that humility is more important than accomplishment. Help me to give You credit for all Your blessings to me.

Reflections

I had breakfast with a friend today. We talked about raising teenage girls. As I listened to her recount interactions with her daughter, I saw myself. My self-reflection didn't end with our breakfast. As I drove away, I thought about how I try to help my girls too much. Sometimes they need understanding and reflection of their feelings, emotions and thoughts more than anything.

My youngest daughter often says, "Just tell me 'no,' Mom. I don't need an explanation."

Perhaps the message God wishes to send through my daughter is to talk less and listen more. My oldest daughter is academically astute, very directed and an all-around good kid with a good head on her shoulders. And yet I can find so many ways to give her input. God keeps quietly reminding me to let her learn, to let her experience life and figure out how to do things, relate to people and grow up.

I find that so hard, because I have this picture of her on my bookshelf: a twelve-month-old baby looking at me with the sweetest face. In some ways, she is still that innocent baby, unaware of the ugly world. I just need to let go of her and trust that God will take care of His child.

I remember my mother telling me that the hardest challenge she had was to let go of her children, to give them back to God. I agree. When my girls were younger, every day that I watched my treasures drive off to school, I prayed that the angels would protect the car and its precious cargo. I still look at them and see Your reflection, Lord.

Thank you, Lord, for sending my reflection through other people so that I can learn and grow in my spiritual journey. I pray that I am a reflection of You.

No Fear

There is no fear in love; but perfect love casts out fear, because fear involves punishment, and the one who fears is not perfected in love.
John 4:18

Do not fear for I am with You; Do not anxiously look about You, for I am your God. I will strengthen You, surely I will help You. Surely I will uphold You with My righteous right hand.
Isaiah 41:10

When I think of my fears, I realize that they take hold when I fail to act on my faith and believe that God is bigger than any problem that I have. Fear does nothing but stifles and causes me to stumble.

As John notes in his gospel, when I act in perfect love and in total dependence on God, I have no fear. And as God said to the Israelites in Isaiah, the Lord is always there to protect me and even fight my battles for me. I don't have to try to slash enemies down with my paltry weapon, for God wields the most powerful sword.

I can think of so many personal relationships in which I feared saying something wrong which might offend someone or make them angry, and I realize that if I act in God's love, I have no reason to fear someone's reaction. I have no fear when following God. This doesn't mean that I can just go around insulting people, I just don't need to worry about it so much. If I focus on Him, His love will shine through me. Besides, some people may get upset with me no matter what I do.

Fear does nothing but distract us from following God in faith. Faith applies to everything I do, including raising children, conducting business, and maintaining relationships. Fear stops me from believing I can achieve what God inspires me to achieve. Fear stifles my growth in relationships because my fear prevents me from trusting people. If we truly believe that God is with us, we can trust others, because if people violate our trust, we have God to hold us when we fall.

"No fear" means that I can let go and let God have control of things. "No fear" provides freedom to live as God's child in the world without reservation as I follow where He leads.

Dear Lord, You are wonderful and full of might, A comfort in a lost and lonely night. Forgive me, Lord, when I do not sing, And proclaim Your glory as heavenly king. Thank you for ruling over fear. Teach me, Lord, Your voice to hear. That I may follow You every day, In faith, as You lead the way.

Patience

Hurry up, Lord, give me patience! He has given me patience by sending situations that have tried my patience. In our fast-paced world, patience is harder and harder to live. I have learned that patience applies in every facet of life.

A businessman, a friend of mine, once helped me with a negotiation. In this negotiation, I wanted to give the other person exactly what he asked for—not really the best idea in the situation. Time went by and my eagerness to come to some agreement grew. Finally, my friend told me to cultivate patience and silence. He was so right. Ultimately the situation turned out better because I didn't jump in and try to force a quick solution that would have resulted in the wrong course of action.

I see many parallels in my walk with the Lord. I want something now. I want God to fix a situation now. If He doesn't do things according to my idea of good timing, I want to jump in and help Him out, as if he needs it! Fortunately, He doesn't always heed my requests to make things happen faster.

Right after my divorce, I couldn't imagine going for

too many years without a serious relationship with a man. God knew better. He knew that I had some things to work out, and that I needed several years to recuperate. He knew my heart well enough to know that I needed to grow before I could get into a dating relationship. God knew the needs of my children. He knew they'd need my full attention as teenagers. I really had no time or emotional resources to sustain a healthy long-term relationship, and God knew it.

God doesn't leave me stranded, though. When I need friends to talk to, to help me along life's road, He sends them. His timing works so much better than mine. God even took away my fear of being in a relationship with a man. Most importantly, He helped me to be more patient and to know that when I do stop and let God have the reins, that He will work out things better than I ever could imagine.

When I guide the children patiently, they react so much calmer. Many times I catch myself telling them to be patient when I'm the one they probably learned impatience from. Their behavior often reflects mine.

When I treat my clients patiently, we have stronger rapport and get our work done better and faster. Once I wrote a training course for a client that had a history of making changes to materials at the last minute. After a while this got very aggravating because it meant that I was essentially working for free and always racing toward a deadline. While I felt like writing a terse e-mail and complaining to the client about the constant changes, I decided not to. Instead, I changed the way I worked with the client.

She often wanted me to start writing material before we had approval from the subject-matter expert, which accounted for more changes than normal. I explained to her that we'd have fewer mistakes in the training materials if we made all the changes at the same time.

This taught me two lessons in patience. First, I had to be patient about finishing the project, and second, to be patient with people who suggest a process that doesn't make sense and doesn't consider my time. By showing her the benefit of making edits all at once, I didn't make her wrong, so her pride remained intact. God helped me be patient with her. Without Him, I'd have shown her my old impatient self.

When I have patience with friends and acquaintances, I hear them better and ultimately build better relationships with them. I recently met the mother of one of my daughter's friends. As a naturally talkative person, I need to take care about overpowering other people. As I spoke to this woman and got to know her, I found that she had a somewhat strained reaction to some of the things I said, as though she thought I disagreed with her. In fact, I only added my thoughts to hers. Rather than decide the problem stemmed from her, I decided to stay quiet and listen to her because she had a lot she needed to say. In that way, hopefully, I demonstrated how God listens to us. He doesn't jump in and give His two cents' worth. He listens to our petitions and hears the desires of our hearts, even if we don't express them. He is incredibly patient. If He were human, He would have given up on me years ago.

When I'm patient with things that don't work, like a

slow garage door opener, it seems to work better. We have two garage door openers. One works fine and the other works occasionally. When I hurriedly stab the garage door opener, it doesn't work very well. When I press it easily and softly, it seems to work better. I think this same principle holds true in communicating with people.

When I hear people quietly and don't try to embellish every conversation, I build stronger and deeper relationships.

God didn't bless me with a natural gift of patience, so God answers my prayers for patience with events that grow patience. As a classroom facilitator for corporate training, I must patiently guide people to new learning. The skill of facilitation lies not so much in telling people what you want them to learn, but rather in asking questions to help them gain new insight and understanding. One time a participant told me that I was the most patient classroom facilitator he had ever met. I chuckled to myself and silently thanked the Lord for working in and with me, because I know I need His strength to make me patient.

Yet those who wait on the Lord will gain new strength; They will mount up with wings like eagles, They will run and not get tired, They will walk and not become weary.
Isaiah 40:31

Thank you, Lord, for sending events that try my patience. Bless you for life's daily events that grow my patience. Help me to continue to become more patient with each day that passes.

The Wellspring

Drink from the wellspring, the wellspring of life,
All of your joys will take over strife.
The song in your heart says to serve your King.
Open your life and your soul will sing.

Refrain:
Stand up and shout for your heavenly King.
Praising His name for the victory He brings.
Claiming so boldly His promise you hear.
Share it with all who are far and near.

Walking by faith and learning to love,
Bring us much closer to the Lord above.
Living within us, He gives us great power.
Showing us how to live every hour.

Ann Lovett Baird
1999

When Our Loved Ones Don't Share Our Faith

I found the passage below in an old journal. Perhaps others who faithfully attend church and try to grow in their Christian journey have a partner or family members who don't share their faith. I hope this chapter helps.

Journal Entry
My heart is saddened Lord, by those who are supposed to be near to my heart, yet are not. I am saddened by one who promises to come with me to church but won't, and who seems to have no concern for me or the importance of my faith.
I do, Lord, bless You and thank You for the blessings You bestow on me. Help me never to forget all that You are to me and how You are the sole purpose for who I am and what I do.

Dear Lord,
You know the depth of my internal loneliness. The joy

and peace that You give never leave me, but in my humanness I need someone to share my faith with. I feel neglected. Please give me patience to wait on You, for You know what I need better than I do. Show me how to share my faith with others who do not trust and know You personally. I am your humble servant.

Daily Journal

The daily journal of my relationship with God helps me to stay focused on Him. Sometimes I go back and read old journal entries and they remind me of how powerfully He has worked in my life. The following are excerpts from some of my old journals.

Journals don't need to be poetic or lyrical. Sometimes I just write something I think God is telling me to do, or an insight he has given me. I hope you'll try it.

Tuesday
Thank you for my precious brothers and sisters in You. Thanks for Your beautiful world, Lord. Help us to be good stewards of the precious gift You have given us.

Wednesday
Dear Lord, Thank you for the gift of health and life. My life with You is a blessing. Your sons and daughters bless me as they shine Your light. You are most precious, my dear Savior. In Your word I can trust, for You are my defense, You are my God. Thank you, Lord, for the blessings You bestow, for the sweet music You give to the

artist's heart. For the vision in the sculptor's hand, for Your divine and perfect plan. Take me in Your arms, Lord, and shelter me with love. Make me a steward, a steward of Your gifts. Teach me to walk in Your light and Your way, and to minister humbly to those in need.

Thursday

I have discovered a need to fellowship with deeply committed Christians, a need I have long ignored. I now pray that God fills that need in a constant way.

Lord, make me able to accept what You have for my life. Show me the cause for inner unrest. Make me patient, Lord, with You and my fellow brothers and sisters. I am weak so You can be strong.

Friday

In the "Final Dream," in Morton Kelsey's *Dreams: A Way to Listen to God,* Kelsey tells a story about a man who was in a coma for two weeks. When the man recovered from the coma, he told of an experience where he was judged by a panel. The sins that the panel judged most harshly were acts of selfishness. Sometimes avoiding selfishness means taking care of myself so that God can use me to serve other's needs.

Give me a merciful heart, O Lord, That I may spread Your peace. Grant the tranquil mind of Yours That I may have Your wisdom. Fill me with Your love, my Lord, That I may share your grace.

Mercy means to share the burden of those who are hurting, to feel their feelings and think their thoughts.

Saturday

Speak to me in my dreams, Lord. Tell me what my heart and soul are saying. Help me to remember my dreams and to wake and record them.

Thank you, Lord, for new friends whom I can pray for and who can pray for me. Thank you for the insights new friends bring. Thank you for the warmth I feel from these new friends.

Sunday

Sing a sweet song,
A kind and refreshing melody,
Free and light, filled with His joy and heartiness.

If you don't keep a journal, consider starting one. Wisdom that God reveals to you may be hard to remember later, at a time when you need it. The journal can help you sort through situations as well.

The Beatitudes

Blessed are the poor in spirit: for theirs is the kingdom of heaven.
Blessed are they that mourn: for they shall be comforted.
Blessed are the meek: for they shall inherit the earth.
Blessed are they who hunger and thirst after righteousness: for they shall be filled.
Blessed are the merciful: for they shall obtain mercy.
Blessed are the pure in heart: for they shall see God.
Blessed are the peacemakers: for they shall be called the children of God.
Blessed are they which are persecuted for righteousness sake: for theirs is the kingdom of heaven.
Matthew 5:3-10

In our world, we often notice people for their accomplishments, for what they do rather than who they are. We look to leaders of countries who are the best at fighting political battles to lead us. We have sayings such as, "When the going gets tough, the tough get going."

Corporations in a state of flux tell their employees to

"deal with it." Life is tough. The toughest corporate negotiators rise to the top. The cleverest attorney has the most accolades. Our children live in a world where their peers walk into schools blasting, killing people who beg for mercy, and murdering peers who profess their faith in God.

Our children have to be tough to survive. Yet God blesses the weak and meek. He promises comfort to those who mourn a terrible loss. Maybe the one who loses the argument isn't really the loser.

Don't get me wrong. Nothing is wrong with success or strong people. However, God doesn't want us to exalt them over the meek, the weak, the downtrodden, or tired. God has such a heart for the hurting, the lonely, the meek soul.

Once I visited with a divorced friend who confessed to feeling ill. She has a delicate build, but has a strong heart for God. I believe she was worn out from holding things together for so long—ten years. I know that God sees her faithful heart and cherishes the fact that she stands for Him. She complains very little. I know of her pain only because of her requests for prayer. I know God views her weakness as precious, her devotion to Him as dear.

I don't mean to suggest that God doesn't favor the successful, but that He doesn't scorn those who don't achieve the level of success that the world values. Nor do I believe that when things go wrong, we should sit around and feel sorry for ourselves and bemoan our plights. God always helps us to handle those times.

These days, teenagers must deal with so much peer pressure. Some of them do things that make them sad and counterproductive. They rip their hearts out trying to be something they're not. They beg for acceptance.

In response, parents abandon them emotionally, sometimes walking away and leaving teenagers to wander in the abyss. Teenagers feel isolated and do crazy things to deal with their pain.

Parents turn their heads and look away when all their children desire is attention. They want someone to say, "You're okay. You don't have to do anything to earn my love or respect."

If only everyone knew the love of God and realized that He will never fail them. No matter what they do, He's no farther than a prayer away. He loves them beyond measure. The Lord will never let go of them, even if they let go of Him. He is the only constant in an ever-changing insanity. He will always protect the people we care about, even if we don't know them well.

Perhaps we see as heroes those who have weathered a rough time and have quietly and meekly suffered life's disappointments. Perhaps we should judge success by spirituality rather than outward accomplishment.

I remember a woman who attended an Episcopal church that I went to in Dallas. I can't even remember her name, but she had a certain quiet genuineness about her that emanated God's love. She always sat in the back of the church and seemed to enter the church as though tiptoeing before God. She possessed a very humble spirit. She spoke very quietly, yet always stood ready to prepare the altar for communion. She served in a humble capacity behind the scenes.

When we ate breakfast after the early church service,

she never joined in the boasting. Many others compared notes about what they planned to accomplish on Monday or recounted how they had conquered this or that client. She always smiled, radiating God's goodness, grace, and quietness. She truly demonstrated the gentleness of God.

Thank you, Lord, for reminding me of the importance of humility. Help me, Lord, to always remember how cherished the humble are. Help me to remember that my greatest riches are in heaven and that everything here on the earth is temporary. Go with me, Lord, as I travel the journey of the Christian life. Walk with me so that I can help others to know the wonder and awe of You. Give me a humble heart so that I notice the quiet, reflective people in the world.

Sing to the Lord a New Song

*Sing to the Lord a new song; Sing to the Lord all the earth. Proclaim good tidings of His salvation from day to day. Tell of His glory among all the nations, His wonderful deeds among all the peoples. For great is the Lord, and greatly to be praised; He is to be feared above all gods. For all the gods of the peoples are idols, But the Lord made the heavens. Splendor and majesty are before Him, Strength and beauty are in His sanctuary.   (*Psalm 96:1-6)

The Lord can refresh our hearts every day if only we let Him. Sometimes I feel lonely or discouraged and I seem to complain to God. When I focus on His blessings to me, I have a renewed sense of lightness in my life.

My office, on the second floor of our home, has a window that looks out on the many trees in the yard, so I get to watch squirrels and birds in the trees. God has painted some of these birds in the most intricate detail. Looking up, I can see the blue and white sky of a fall afternoon filtering through the leaves on the trees. This view constantly reminds me to sing a new and rejoicing song to God in my heart every day.

Sometimes I actually sing sitting at my desk. Lifting my voice to God in song is the best medicine for sadness or whatever disappointment I have. The words and music help me focus on the big picture and realize that this day, this month, this year, are only specks in the scheme of God's universe and eternity.

Tomorrow or the next day, this pain, hurt or disappointment may have vanished. If I don't feel like singing, playing music that exalts God helps tremendously. My mom always taught me to play praise music to raise my spirits.

I find it so amazing that the same God who created earth, awesome in its beauty and splendor, a God worthy of our fear and praise, loves each one of us as His precious children. He sees each one of us unique and special, and sees our qualities better than we do. He sees our hurt, pain and weakness and loves the humblest parts of us. We can turn to Him with grateful hearts every day, for He is there, constant and kind, loving and understanding, providing us a new verse of a song every day.

Thank you, Lord, for the new song You give us every day. Bless You for the beauty of Your creation and the creatures in it.

Journeying Forward

I sincerely hope that this diary will inspire you to follow God daily, walking in faith, listening for, and diligently acting on His call for you. He calls us all to various missions and activities based on the gifts He has given us. May your heart overflow with joy and gratefulness for His unswerving commitment to you, and may you always be blessed for diligently serving your Lord.

(Deuteronomy 28:1-8)

To order additional copies of
*** Diary of an Everyday Christian ***

Name _____

Address _____

_____

_____

$12.95 (tax included) x _____ copies = ____

Please add $3.50 postage and handling
for first book and $1.25 for each
additional book _____

Total amount due:

Please send check or money order for books to:
*** Special Delivery Books ***
WordWright Business Park
46561 State Highway 118
Alpine, TX 79830

**For a complete catalog of books,
visit our site at**
http://www.SpecialDeliveryBooks.com

LaVergne, TN USA
14 September 2010
196981LV00001B/5/P